Much More

to

Christmas

Written and Illustrated by

Brenda K. Hendricks

This book is dedicated to

Dorothy Pollock
and
Marsha Hubler

Thanks for your suggestions, encouragement,
and especially for your patience.

Much More to Christmas

Text and Illustrations Copyright © 2014 by Brenda Hendricks
Published by Two Small Fish Publications,
109 W. Market Street, Freeburg, PA 17827
Manufactured in the United States of America

www.twosmallfish.org
www.myquotesofencouragement.com
www.brendakhendricks.blogspot.com

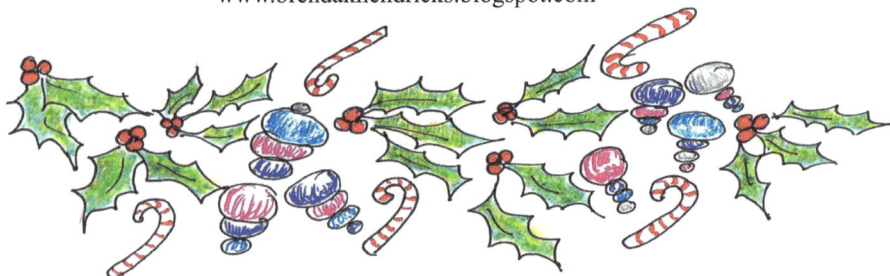

We all enjoy presents
with ribbons and tags,

Giving and getting
gifts, boxes, and bags;

So, what shall I give? Do I dare ask for more?

And what do I spend on each gift at the store?

I've shopped, and I ache
from my head to my feet,
I'm tired of smiling
at folks whom I meet;

Happy I'll
be when the
garland's all hung,
I wish it was o'er, and the
last song was sung.

Then, with my
bustling, I've
thought,

Is it true?

Could Christmas
mean much more

to me and to you?

Door bells ringing

Laughing and singing

Friends and caring

Memory sharing

Talking, joking

Tender rib poking

Susan and Joe

Beneath mistletoe

Good will greetings

Parties, church meetings.

But there is much, much more; I give you my word;

There's much more to Christmas, or haven't you heard?

An angel met Mary,

the virgin and blessed

**Then stood before Joseph
to cheer and impress,**

"Take Mary to wife and the child as your own;

He one day will rule from his heavenly throne."

Humble shepherds watched

sheep late that night,

While angels chorused

God's promise with delight;

The glory of God turned

the dark into day

While Jesus the Babe

fell asleep on the hay;

The Savior became a compassionate man

With marvelous healing in both of his hands.

Mercy and grace

Glorified His face

People believed

Miracles received

Burdens lifted

Tempers Shifted

A crown of thorns

Soldiers' hateful scorns

Hung on a cross
Suffering and loss

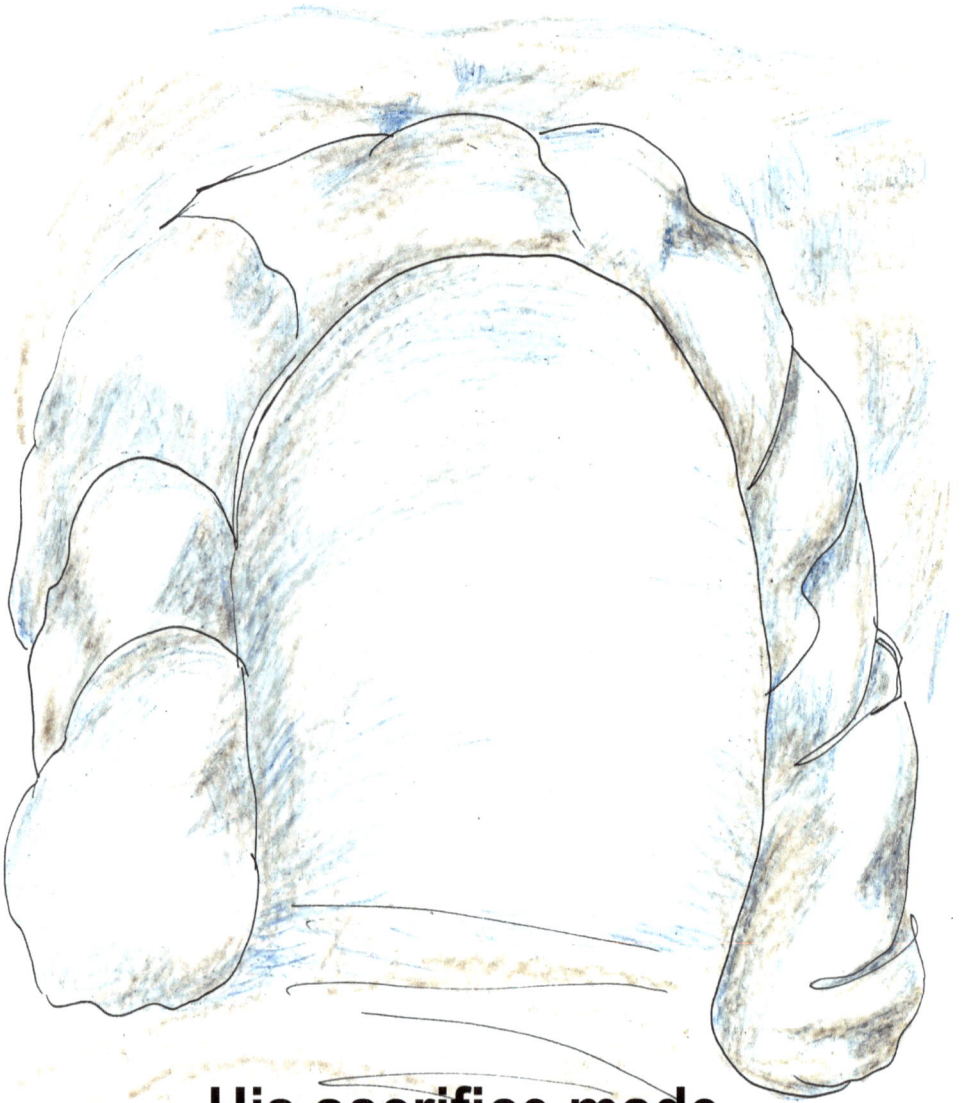

His sacrifice made,

he was laid in a tomb;

The whole Earth did mourn
over three days of gloom.

But then God, His Father, said, "Come out, my Son! Rejoice and be glad for the victory's won!"

The first Christmas Day
the best gift had been giv'n,
And Jesus still lives, so
my sins are forgiven.

As long as I live, I will

spend all my days

Rejoicing and singing and
shouting His praise;

I've seen it, I've felt it,

I know it is true,

Yes, Christmas means
much more to me

and to you.

Other Books by
Brenda K. Hendricks

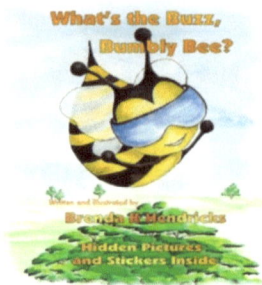

Flying high is Bumbly Bee's favorite thing to do until he hears the latest neighborhood buzz. Bumblebee wings are too small to carry their heavy bodies." Will his friends' comments ground him for life? Or will he answer "What's the buzz?" with a stronger trust in God?

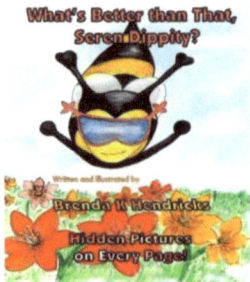

Every plump-with-pollen daylily in the field belongs to Seren Dippity. What's better than that? But she's not sharing. Will she learn to stop stinging and scaring and start singing and sharing before she loses all her friends?

Purchase them on Amazon. Available for Kindle

Follow Brenda on Face Book and Twitter

Join her at www.myquotesof encouragement

and www.brendakhendricks.blogspot.com

www.ingramcontent.com/pod-product-compliance
Lightning Source LLC
Chambersburg PA
CBHW041818040426
42452CB00001B/19